MEASURING AND COMPARING

How Tall is Tall?
Comparing Structures

Vic Parker

www.raintreepublishers.co.uk
Visit our website to find out more information about Raintree books.

To order:
☎ Phone 0845 6044371
🖹 Fax +44 (0) 1865 312263
🖥 Email myorders@raintreepublishers.co.uk

Customers from outside the UK please telephone +44 1865 312262

Raintree is an imprint of Capstone Global Library Limited, a company incorporated in England and Wales having its registered office at 7 Pilgrim Street, London, EC4V 6LB – Registered company number: 6695582

Text © Capstone Global Library Limited 2011
First published in hardback in 2011
The moral rights of the proprietor have been asserted.

Edited by Nancy Dickmann, Rebecca Rissman, and Sian Smith
Designed by Victoria Allen
Picture research by Hannah Taylor
Original illustrations © Capstone Global Library Ltd
Original illustrations by Victoria Allen
Production by Victoria Fitzgerald
Originated by Dot Gradations Ltd
Printed and bound in China by South China Printing Company Ltd

ISBN 978 0 431 00683 3
14 13 12 11 10
10 9 8 7 6 5 4 3 2 1

British Library Cataloguing in Publication Data
Parker, Victoria.
How tall is tall? : comparing structures. -- (Measuring and comparing)
1. Tall buildings--Juvenile literature. 2. Measurement--Juvenile literature.
I. Title II. Series
530.8-dc22

Acknowledgements
The author and publisher are grateful to the following for permission to reproduce copyright material: Alamy Images pp.10 (© vario images GmbH & Co.KG), 12 (© inga spence), 18 (© JLImages); © Capstone Publishers pp.4, 8, 26, 27 (Karon Dubke); Corbis p.24 (epa/ Peter Kneffel); istockphoto p.20 (© Henryk Sadura); Photolibrary pp.5, 6 (age fotostock/ P Narayan), 7 (Len Delessio); shutterstock pp.14 (© BEEE), 16 (© upthebanner); Wayne Howes p.22.

Photographs used to create silhouettes: shutterstock, child (© angel digital), house (© Andrii Syneok), pylon (© Fica), London Eye (© Cihan Demirok, CIDEPIX), Golden Gate Bridge (© Slobodan Djajic), Eiffel Tower (© Ints Vikmanis), Willis Tower (© jamaican).

Cover photograph of the skyline from Brooklyn Heights promenade, New York reproduced with permission of Photolibrary (Steve Dunwell).

Every effort has been made to contact copyright holders of material reproduced in this book. Any omissions will be rectified in subsequent printings if notice is given to the publisher.

Disclaimer
All the Internet addresses (URLs) given in this book were valid at the time of going to press. However, due to the dynamic nature of the Internet, some addresses may have changed or ceased to exist since publication. While the author and publisher regret any inconvenience this may cause readers, no responsibility for any such changes can be accepted by either the author or the publisher.

Contents

Words appearing in the text in bold, **like this**,
are explained in the glossary.

Measuring height

The height of something is how tall it is. To measure height you can use a ruler, wall chart, tape measure, or measuring stick. These are marked in millimetres (mm), centimetres (cm), and metres (m).

A door handle is often about 1 metre high.

There are some things we can't reach the top of, such as buildings. To measure the height of buildings, experts use special tools which look rather like cameras.

This **surveyor** is measuring the height of the building.

Why do people build tall structures?

Tall buildings can be useful. This is because they can fit hundreds or even thousands of people inside, without taking up much ground. This is helpful in crowded cities.

The city of Shanghai, in China, has many tall skyscrapers.

Tall structures can be impressive and beautiful. The Statue of Liberty stands in New York Harbor in the USA. People on ships heading for New York can see the statue from a long way off.

Some people think the Statue of Liberty looks like it is welcoming people to New York.

Measure your height

Have you ever measured how tall you are? Compared to a younger brother or sister, you might be tall. But how tall is tall?

You can measure yourself in centimetres or metres.

A house with two floors is often about 7½ metres high. If you and five of your friends stood on top of each other, you wouldn't quite reach the top of a house.

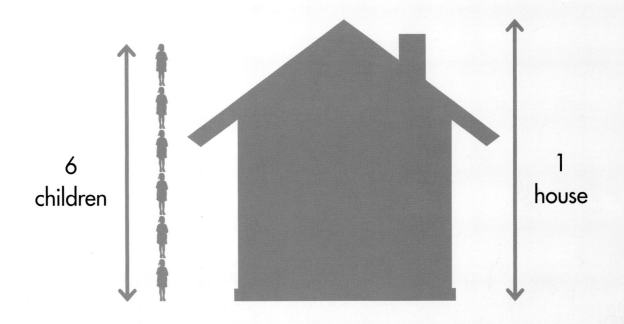

6 children

1 house

What is taller than a house? ➡

Electricity pylons

An **electricity pylon** is taller than a house. Electricity pylons are made from steel. They carry cables for **electricity** from place to place.

Electricity is the energy that powers equipment such as lights, televisions, and computers.

A regular electricity pylon is about 50 metres tall. This is higher than six houses on top of each other.

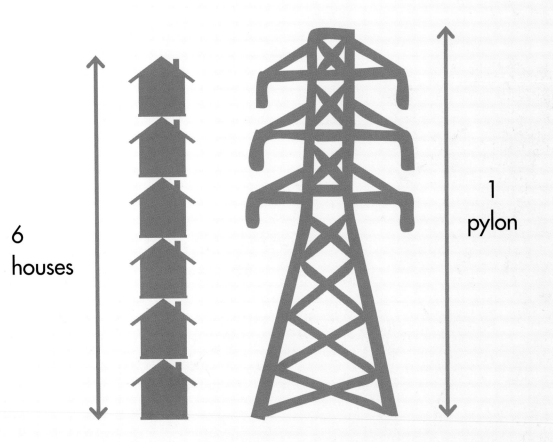

6 houses

1 pylon

What is taller than an electricity pylon? ➡

Wind turbines

A wind turbine is taller than an **electricity pylon**.
Wind turbines are like giant windmills. They use
the power of the wind to make **electricity**.

A group of wind turbines
is called a wind farm.

A wind turbine can be around 90 metres tall. This is nearly as high as two electricity pylons on top of each other.

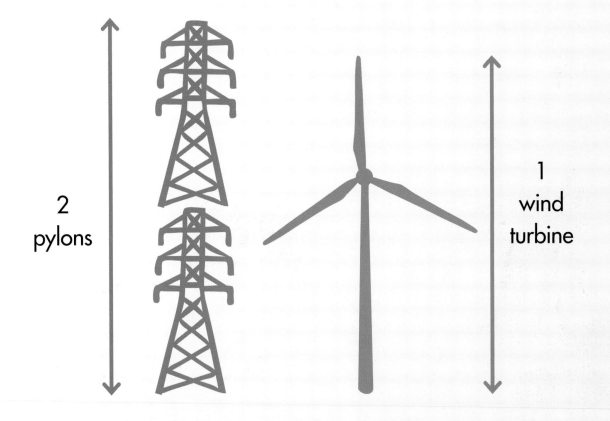

2 pylons

1 wind turbine

What is taller than a wind turbine? ➡

The London Eye

Fun rides such as **roller coasters** and **Ferris wheels** can be taller than a **wind turbine**. This giant Ferris wheel is the London Eye in London.

The London Eye can carry 800 people at once.

The London Eye moves slowly, so people inside the **capsules** can admire the view over the city. It is 135 metres tall. This is as tall as one and a half wind turbines.

1½ wind turbines

1 London Eye

What is taller than the London Eye? →

The Golden Gate Bridge

The Golden Gate Bridge is taller than the London Eye. The Golden Gate Bridge is in San Francisco Bay in the USA.

Every day, about 107,000 **vehicles** cross the Golden Gate Bridge.

The towers on the Golden Gate Bridge rise 227 metres above the water. If you put one and a half London Eyes on top of each other, the Golden Gate Bridge would still be taller!

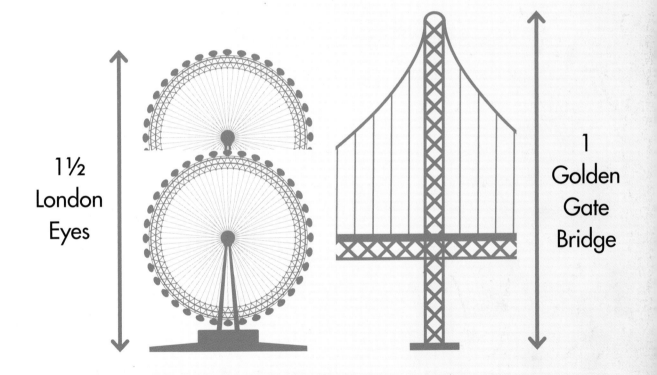

1½ London Eyes

1 Golden Gate Bridge

What is taller than the Golden Gate Bridge? ➡

The Eiffel Tower

The Eiffel Tower is taller than the Golden Gate Bridge. The Eiffel Tower is in Paris, in France. It was built to look impressive and to let people sightsee over the city.

The Eiffel Tower was built over 120 years ago.

The Eiffel Tower is 324 metres tall. If there were a **wind turbine** on top of the Golden Gate Bridge, the Eiffel Tower would still be taller!

1 wind turbine

1 Golden Gate Bridge

1 Eiffel Tower

What is taller than the Eiffel Tower? ➡

The Willis Tower

A **skyscraper** called the Willis Tower is taller than the Eiffel Tower. The Willis Tower is in Chicago in the USA. The Willis Tower is full of offices. **Radio** and **television** **signals** are also sent from the tower.

The Willis Tower used to be known as the Sears Tower.

When it was built in 1973, the Willis Tower was the tallest skyscraper in the world. It is 442 metres tall. This is nearly one and a half times as tall as the Eiffel Tower.

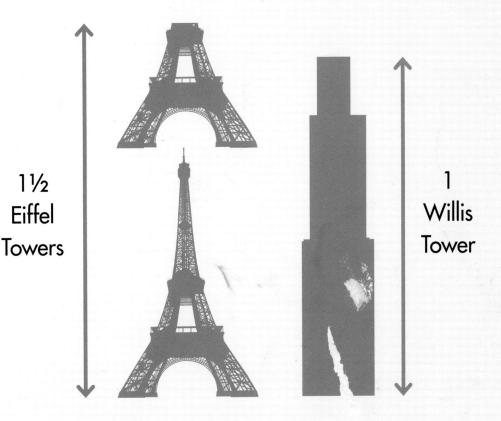

1½
Eiffel
Towers

1
Willis
Tower

What is taller than the Willis Tower? ➡

The KVLY-TV mast

The KVLY-TV **mast** is taller than the Willis Tower. The mast is in the state of North Dakota, in the USA. It is used by a TV channel to send **television signals**.

The KVLY-TV mast was completed in 1963.

KVLY-TV mast

The KVLY-TV mast is 629 metres tall. This means that if you put the London Eye on top of the Willis Tower, the KVLY-TV mast would still be taller!

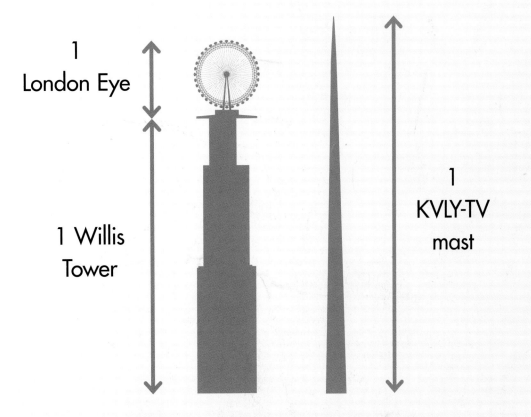

1
London Eye

1 Willis
Tower

1
KVLY-TV
mast

What is taller than the KVLY-TV mast? ➡

The world's tallest structure

Burj Khalifa is taller than the KVLY-TV **mast**. This **skyscraper** is in Dubai in the Middle East. It is full of offices, apartments, and hotels. Burj Khalifa is the tallest structure in the whole world – so far.

Burj Khalifa has the world's fastest lifts.

Burj Khalifa is 818 metres tall. This is far taller than the KVLY-TV mast. It would take you and about 704 of your friends, standing on each other's heads, to reach the top of Burj Khalifa!

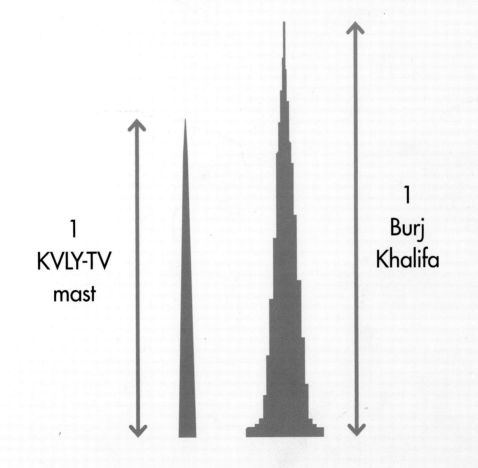

1
KVLY-TV
mast

1
Burj
Khalifa

Measuring activity

Things you will need: toilet rolls of the same size, building blocks of the same height, a tape measure, a pencil, and paper.

1. Measure the height of a door handle by stacking building blocks on top of each other. Write down how many are needed to reach the door handle.

(2) Measure the height of the door handle again by stacking toilet rolls on top of each other. Write down how many toilet rolls this takes.

(3) Measure the height of the door handle using a tape measure. Write down the height of the door handle in centimetres.

Find out: Does the door handle sound taller in building blocks, toilet rolls, or centimetres? Even though they sound different, all these measurements are showing the same height.

Tall quiz and facts

Remember

10 millimetres (mm) = 1 centimetre (cm)
100 centimetres (cm) = 1 metre (m)

Very small heights are measured in millimetres (mm).
Larger heights are measured in centimetres (cm).
Big heights are measured in metres (m).

Quiz

1. What unit would you use to measure the height of a fly?

    a) millimetres   b) centimetres   c) metres

2. What unit would you use to measure the height of a lighthouse?

    a) millimetres   b) centimetres   c) metres

3. What unit would you use to measure the height of a window?

    a) millimetres   b) centimetres   c) metres

Answers: 1 = a   2 = c   3 = b

Tall facts

- Giraffes are the world's tallest land creatures. A giraffe can be more than 5½ metres tall.

- A fireman's ladder can be about 33 metres tall.

- The world's tallest lighthouse is the Yokohama lighthouse in Japan. It is 106 metres tall.

- Hyperion is the tallest tree in the world. It is a coast redwood tree growing in California, USA. It is 115 metres tall.

- The world's tallest clock tower is at the NTT Docomo Yoyogi Building in Tokyo, Japan. It is 240 metres tall.

- The world's tallest **roller coaster** is Kingda Ka in New Jersey, USA. It is nearly 139 metres tall.

Glossary

capsule egg-shaped compartment for carrying people in

electricity energy that people use to make lights, televisions, computers, and other machines work

electricity pylon large structure that carries electricity cables

Ferris wheel type of ride shaped like a huge wheel with places for people to sit, while they are carried round

mast tall pole used to hold up a radio or television aerial

radio signals invisible waves that radio equipment can pick up and turn into sounds

roller coaster type of ride where people move along a twisting track at high speeds for fun

skyscraper extremely tall building for people to live or work in

surveyor person whose job it is to measure buildings and landscapes

television signals invisible waves that television equipment can pick up and turn into pictures and sounds

vehicle any type of transport that carries people or things from place to place. Cars, bicycles, and trucks are all vehicles.

wind turbine structure shaped like a large windmill. Wind turbines use the power of the wind to make electricity.

Find out more

Books

Incredible Skyscrapers, Geoff Barker
(Franklin Watts, 2009)

See Inside Famous Buildings, Rob Lloyd Jones
(Usborne, 2009)

Websites

skyscraperpage.com/diagrams/?searchID=200
Visit this website to compare the tallest buildings in
the world!

www.pbs.org/wgbh/buildingbig/skyscraper
Find out fun facts about skyscrapers and try the
skyscraper challenge on this website.

www.skyscraperpicture.com
This website is packed with photos and information
about skyscrapers in different countries.

Index